COOKING WITH THE CHOIR

UNFORGETTABLE
RECIPES

FAMILY FAVORITES AND THE STORIES BEHIND THEM

Cooking with the Choir: Unforgettable Recipes
Family Favorites and the Stories Behind Them

Published by
Beacon Mount Publishing
Victoria, BC, Canada

Editors:
Andrea Warner
Erica Phare-Bergh

Cover and interior design by Stephanie Anderson at Alt 19 Creative

ISBN: 978-1-988082-32-5

Printed and bound in the United States of America.

www.voicesinmotionchoirs.org

VOICES IN **MOTION**
A intergenerational choir for adults with memory
loss, their caregivers, friends and students

THANKS TO OUR SPONSORS

A special thank you to our supporters and sponsors for their generosity and for believing in us.

FIRST MEMORIAL
FUNERAL SERVICES

INTRODUCTION

This cookbook is story driven. It is written by choir members from Voices in Motion.

The intergenerational choirs of Voices in Motion are for adults with memory loss, their caregivers and friends, and high school students.

In 2017, Voices in Motion started as a research project out of the University of Victoria. The choirs continue to provide a meaningful, healthy and effective intervention for those on a journey with dementia and their caregivers.

You can read some of the amazing results from our research at the back of this book.

Why a cookbook by a choir? Because, we are a community of people with fascinating stories.

But where do you begin to share stories that hold deep meaning and connection?

Our choir members with dementia often speak about the importance of support from their family members and close friends. This support, encouragement and joy was often experienced during shared meals together. We thought, "Why not compile a cookbook in which our choristers could share their favourite family recipes and the memorable stories that go with them?"

Thus, the adventure began.

Our choir members dug deep into their favourite recipes, wrote the stories surrounding them and took pictures of the finished products to create this wonderful cookbook – *Cooking with the Choir: Unforgettable Recipes*.

We hope that as you make these recipes, and as you sit down around the table to enjoy them, you will also enjoy learning about the stories behind these dishes. Perhaps you will be inspired to reach out to someone in your community experiencing memory loss, and maybe invite them over for a meal.

Thanks for Cooking with the Choir.

Rick Bergh
Executive Director, Voices in Motion
www.voicesinmotionchoirs.org

VOICES IN MOTION
A intergenerational choir for adults with memory loss, their caregivers, friends and students

CONTENTS

THE RECIPES

BAKED ARTICHOKE DIP

Contributed By: Wendy Casey

Picture my best friend, Donna, who is preparing for a holiday party. Donna is meticulous, everything she does is to perfection, and her friends and family always look forward to being the recipient of a royal invite to one of her parties. One year she added to her famous appetizer spread my Artichoke Dip.

She called me a few days after the party to tell me the appetizer was a complete failure and it had turned into something like a bowl full of runny curdled pablum. We dissected the recipe by reviewing the ingredients, size of dish and oven temperature to see if she had measured wrong or forgotten something, and we both agreed that she had done everything correctly.

Determined to have a success, Donna decided to make the Dip again and carefully followed the recipe, only to have the same result. I was baffled. We dissected the recipe and ingredients again and so far, everything sounded correct. I then asked her to explain to me what steps she did from beginning to end. It all sounded good until she said, "…and then I covered the dish with tin foil."

"Wait…what? No! No lid or covering the dish with tin foil!! The dish must bake uncovered otherwise the steam stays in the dish with the other ingredients and ruins it!" So there you have it. Bake this dish uncovered until light brown and bubbly. This fantastic appetizer is hot and cheesy and is delicious on crackers, sliced bread, or mixed in with pasta….so says Donna!

INGREDIENTS

1 can artichoke hearts, drained

1 cup mayonnaise (not Miracle Whip)

1 cup fresh grated Parmesan cheese (not dried from a shaker tin)

1–2 cloves garlic

DIRECTIONS

1) Pre-heat oven to 350°F.

2) I like using a food processor to mix it all in a few short bursts, but you could easily chop the artichokes, use a garlic press, and mix in a bowl. Put into an appropriate-sized baking dish and bake at 350°F until bubbling and brown on top.

3) Add ½ cup lightly steamed and chopped spinach, water chestnuts, or some crab to make this appetizer even better!

SHRIMP & CHEESE APPETIZERS

Contributed by: Wendy & Ken Patterson

We got this recipe from Carol, a wonderful friend and neighbour, who lived two houses away from us in the Lansdowne area of Edmonton when we were both raising our families. Each family had two children and since neither had relatives in the city, we shared many meals and special occasions. They were Maritimers and taught us how to "live in the moment" and enjoy fish. Occasionally they had fresh lobster or crab flown in from Nova Scotia which they shared—we have great memories of drawn butter dripping down our chins.

Entertaining in those days when we were young and energetic always included a starter, a main and a decadent dessert. We weren't as bright as the young people nowadays who have potlucks to share the work around! Carol was the source of many of my good tasting but easily prepared recipes.

We've taken these starters to many functions and invariably people request the recipe. Any appetizer that can be made ahead, with little fuss is a hit with most cooks. We have happy memories of relaxing, nursing a glass of wine, and munching on these savoury morsels. These starters are easy, tasty, freezable, and the recipe makes 72 pieces!

INGREDIENTS

1 tin cocktail
    shrimp (106g)
2 ½ Tbsp Hellman's
    mayonnaise
½ cup margarine
    (hard, not the
    spreadable kind)
1 tub MacLaren's Imperial sharp
    cheddar (230g)
1 clove garlic, minced
½–1 tsp chili paste or pinch of cayenne pepper
    (optional but gives a little bite)
1 package English muffins

DIRECTIONS

1) Soften margarine and cheddar and mix well. Add mayo, chili paste (or cayenne), minced garlic. Drain shrimp, rinse under cold water, pat dry. Mash shrimp with a fork. Add to cheese mixture.
2) Slice English muffins horizontally into 2 pieces. Spread shrimp/cheese mixture on cut surfaces.
3) Cut each piece into half and then each half into 3 triangles (use slightly moistened sharp knife). Each muffin half makes 6 appetizers.
4) If using immediately, place triangles on broiler pan and broil until lightly browned. Place each browned appetizer on a paper towel so it's not too messy for finger food and then serve. If freezing, place on cookie sheet and once frozen place in freezer bag. Broil from frozen state.

COCONUT CURRY LENTIL SOUP

Contributed by: Erica Phare-Bergh

'm an avid scrapbooker. I've made scrapbooks—for important family birthday milestones, ABC books for my grandkids, a personal scrapbook and lots and lots of cards. When I lived in Montreal and Calgary, I used to go on retreats with other devoted scrapbookers. That was my form of play—and it was practical too.

One wintery weekend in Alberta, I headed off to Santcum Retreat Centre in Caroline, AB, to do some scrapbooking. There were probably 25 women at the event. I'm sure it was a lovely time and I got some projects completed, but the most memorable part of the weekend for me was the soup that we had for Saturday lunch. I'm pretty sure that I went up for seconds—maybe even thirds. Empty bowl in hand, I barged into the back kitchen and asked for the recipe. The cook wrote it out on a napkin for me—so the measurements are kind of approximate in this recipe. Regardless, the result is always delicious.

It's probably my favourite soup and I make it often. It's quite filling and tastes great with a fresh bun on a chilly day.

INGREDIENTS

1 lb lentils (I use orange lentils)
28 oz can diced tomatoes, with liquid
6 cups chicken or veggie stock*
2–3 large carrots, chopped
2–3 stocks celery, chopped
1 Tbsp dried parsley
1 Tbsp curry (or more if you like curry)
1–2 tsp garlic powder
2 tsp oregano
1–2 cans coconut milk**

* I use a box of chicken stock = 4 cups, plus water and chicken stock concentrate, like OXO.
** I use only one to keep it lighter. You can also use powered coconut milk in water.

DIRECTIONS

Bring to a boil then simmer for 1 ½ hours. Add a little water if soup is too thick. The recipe makes a large pot of soup. Freezes well.

GRACE'S FANTASTIC TOMATO SOUP

Contributed by: Deanna Dillabaugh

INGREDIENTS

¼ lb. butter or margarine

1 cup chopped celery

1 cup chopped onion

1 cup chopped carrots

⅓ cup all-purpose flour

1 can tomato soup

3–4 fresh tomatoes, sliced

2 tsp sugar (optional)*

1 tsp basil

1 tsp marjoram

2 bay leaves

4 cups chicken broth

2 cups whipping cream (optional)*

½ tsp paprika

½ tsp white pepper

Salt to taste

* I should have noted that I never put in the sugar or cream as it doesn't need it, in my opinion.

This is our "go-to" soup and always receives many compliments, so I hope you try it out and like it as much as we do.

Thank you to Grace, whom this recipe came from. Grace is my daughter's mother-in-law who is not only an amazing cook but is kind, thoughtful and full of laughs. In our family, soup has always been a favourite. Food brings us together, whether it's family, friends, neighbours or communities.

DIRECTIONS

1) Melt butter or margarine in a large saucepan. Sauté celery, onion, and carrots until tender. Stir in flour. Cook 2 minutes, stirring constantly. Add tomato soup, fresh tomatoes, sugar (if using), basil, marjoram, bay leaves and chicken broth. Cover and simmer 30 minutes, stirring occasionally.

2) Discard bay leaves. Purée ⅓ of soup at a time in a blender or use a hand-held immersion blender. Add cream (if using), paprika, curry powder and pepper. Stir to blend. Add salt to taste.

3) Serve hot or cold. May be refrigerated for several days or frozen in an airtight container for 4 to 6 months.

SPINACH DIP

Contributed by: Jörg & Tish Stangl

We frequently make this dip when we are invited out somewhere and need to bring something. It's usually quickly devoured. When our son was young, we made it a tradition to go out for dinner on Friday evenings. One of the spots we frequented was Milestones and this spinach dip was one of our favorite choices from their menu (but sometimes left us too full to eat our main meal). Tish eventually found a recipe for it and it's become a favorite with all our friends as well.

INGREDIENTS

1 cup mozzarella cheese, grated

1 cup parmesan cheese, freshly grated

1 cup mayonnaise

Pepper

15 oz can or 1 cup artichokes (drained and cut up)

2 cloves garlic, minced

4 oz cream cheese

10 oz package frozen chopped spinach, thawed and drained

DIRECTIONS

Combine all ingredients in an oven-proof dish. Bake in 325°F oven for 20 minutes. Serve with favorite crackers or warm baguette.

TOMATO AND SCRAMBLED EGG NOODLES

Contributed by: Amy Li

This dish was made by my dad for my mom when they were still teens, deeply in love. My parents met at their art high school and went to the same art university together. My mom had always secretly liked my dad. However, she really had no confidence to tell him so. They would often do sketching practice and assignments in his dorm.

One evening, when they were sketching, my mom suddenly started to feel sick and her fever spiked. Seeing her almost pass out, my dad unhesitatingly carried her on his back and ran to the hospital, which was about two miles away from his dorm. After they gave my mom an injection, he carried her back to his dorm and had her lie down on his bed. Very content, she soon fell asleep. When she woke up, there was the smell of cooking in the room. This was unusual, since food, drinks and stoves weren't allowed in dorms back then! My dad and his friend had stolen a stove and some ingredients from other friends so that he could make my mom this dish. After she finished eating, he carried my mom back to her dorm, his jacket covering her shoulders. The very next day, he confessed that he really liked her and they began dating. She was 17 and he was 16.

INGREDIENTS

1 large tomato
2 large eggs or 3 small eggs
2 portions of noodles*
1 ½ Tbsp of ketchup
2 cloves of garlic, sliced
1 Tbsp of water
Vegetable oil (preferably not oil with a strong
    flavour, like olive oil)
2 scallions
Handful of cilantro
Salt & pepper to taste
* You can use any kind of noodles you like,
    preferably long, thin, stretchy ones you can get
    from any Asian store.

DIRECTIONS

1) Crack the eggs into a mixing bowl, add 1 tablespoon of water into the bowl and whisk until the yolks and the whites are well mixed. Add salt and pepper.
2) Wash the tomato and chop into small chunks.
3) Chop fresh garlic cloves and scallions into thin slices.
4) Heat oil in a sauté pan on medium heat (VERY IMPORTANT NOTICE: If the temperature is too high, when you put the ingredients in IT WILL CREATE A TON OF SMOKE).
5) Add eggs and stir-fry until cooked. Put them into a bowl for later use.
6) Sauté tomato until soft. Add ketchup and mix well. Add water and simmer.
7) Combine scrambled eggs and tomato mixture.
8) Boil noodles. Drain. Serve in a bowl. Top with egg and tomato mixture. Garnish with cilantro leaves. And you're done!

BLACKENED SALMON
Contributed by: Susan & Caitlyn Ledohowski

During the past several weeks my mom has been looking at an Earls' cookbook. Specifically, at their recipe for blackened salmon. Just like any recipe, my mom did not follow the recipe word-for-word. She simply takes inspiration from it. Because she knows the taste of different ingredients and their various combinations, she can easily improvise a delicious dish. She rarely memorizes her own improvisations. She usually makes something slightly different each time. However, I was her assistant chef for this fateful day.

It was my first attempt at preparing the spices that would be rubbed onto the fish. While I took some of my mom's advice for adding the spices, I mostly followed the recipe word-for-word. This is when I made a disastrous mistake… When we finally served the salmon, my youngest sister took one bite and stared blankly at her food. We asked her what was wrong. Hot spice! It was the bane of her existence. Her eyes watered as she forced herself to eat it. It was actually a fantastic salmon, but clearly it didn't suit everyone's preferences!

Only recently have I decided to occasionally help cook meals. I tend to make mistakes due to my lack of expertise, but the dish found the approval of each family member. I was determined to succeed in order to fix my previous failure. For my second attempt, I heavily consulted my mom about the kind and quantity of spices I should include for the dish. I proceeded to record the ingredients on a notepad for future reference. For the dish, we wanted to retain the tasty flavour from our initial attempt while minimizing the spiciness. It was finally time to serve our dish… My sister hesitated. And she took a bite. The tinkered recipe received her golden stamp of approval! After the meal, our family was looking forward to eating it again. What can I say? It is now a family favourite.

INGREDIENTS
SPICE RUB:
1 tsp fine salt
½ tsp smoked paprika
½ tsp hot garlic seasoning
¼ tsp Montreal Steak Spice
⅛ tsp white pepper
2 Tbsp thyme
2 Tbsp rosemary
2 Tbsp oregano
2 Tbsp garlic powder
Tip: Adding salt or hot spices (such as smoked paprika and white pepper) are optional. It depends on your preferences!
OTHER COOKING INGREDIENTS:
Salmon
Olive oil or Butter

DIRECTIONS

1) Combine the spices in a bowl until they are equally distributed. Option: You can further blend the spices in a blender, so the mixture is more consistent.
2) Rub the spice equally on all sides of each salmon piece.
3) Pour olive oil or put butter in the pan. Heat up your pan to 'Medium Low' or 'Medium.'
4) When the olive oil or butter starts to simmer, place the salmon pieces in the pan.
5) Leave the salmon for 3–5 minutes on the top and 3–5 minutes on the bottom, until each side is slightly burnt.
6) The blackened salmon is ready to serve!

BUFFET MUSTARD CHICKEN

Contributed by: Erica Phare-Bergh

When I lived in Montreal—and was still a career spinster—I had a housemate named Jen. She was a really good cook and had great recipes that were both delicious and quick. While this wasn't one of the ones that she used to make, it did appear in the recipe card box at my wedding shower. Each person was asked to write up their favourite recipe to get me started on my own recipe box. Jen knew that I liked quick, yummy, healthy and easy recipes. So this was her offering in that box. I still have the recipe card in her handwriting. It's been a keeper. Served hot or cold, it's super delicious and super easy. It tastes great chopped up and thrown on a salad or over rice. Every time I make it, I think of my dear friend, Jennifer.

INGREDIENTS

½ butter

¼ cup Dijon mustard

2 Tbsp prepared mustard

½ cup honey

2 tsp curry powder

2 tsp lemon or lime juice

1 tsp salt

⅛ tsp garlic powder

4–5 cups raw chicken breasts, cubed

DIRECTIONS

1) Melt first 8 ingredients together in a saucepan at medium heat.
2) Place chicken in a casserole dish and pour melted honey mustard sauce over it and mix together.
3) Cook covered at 350°F for 45–50 minutes.
4) Serve over rice or serve cold over salad.
5) You could also use chicken thighs.

I've also used the slow cooker on occasion and that works too—just be careful that there is enough moisture so chicken isn't dry.

CHILI CON CARNE

Contributed by: Geraldine Meagher

really like one pot meals and this one is a staple in our household. The beauty of this recipe is that it can be adjusted to fit everyone's likes and tastes—add more or less spice, add some red or green peppers, try out some different bean combinations. This one has been adapted from a recipe used in a Soup Kitchen that I used to help out with in White Rock, BC. Obviously, their recipe was for a much bigger crowd; this one will feed about 6. It actually tastes better the next day and leftovers can be frozen for a quick nutritious meal on a busy day.

INGREDIENTS

1 lb lean ground beef
3 hot Italian sausage links, casing removed (I like the ones from Costco)
1 onion diced
2 cloves garlic, diced
2 Tbsp dried oregano
1 can tomato paste
1 can diced tomatoes
2 medium sweet potatoes, peeled and diced (optional)
1 can chickpeas
1 can red kidney beans
1 can black beans
2 Tbsp chili powder
2 Tbsp chili flakes
Salt & pepper to taste

DIRECTIONS

1) In a large pot over medium heat cook ground beef, sausage, onion, garlic and oregano together until browned. Remove fat as desired.
2) Add tomato paste and diced tomatoes, stir until well combined.
3) Add sweet potato. Drain the chickpeas, kidney beans and black beans before adding to pot. Add in chili spices and salt & pepper to taste.
4) Simmer over medium heat for at least 1 hour.
5) Serve with crusty bread or rice. Enjoy!

FAR EAST CHICKEN

Contributed by: Pam DeMontigny

I feel very fortunate that in my senior years my husband and I live near two of our children. We take turns hosting Sunday dinners at each other's house. The evening usually includes music and games.

One of my mom's famous recipes that has been passed down two generations and remains a family favourite…as a matter of fact, I'm mixing the sauce today to take with us tomorrow when we go for a long-awaited family week at a beach house. Hope you enjoy Far East Chicken as much as our family does!

INGREDIENTS

6–8 pieces of chicken
¼ cup honey
¼ cup oil
⅔ cup soya sauce
1 clove garlic, crushed
1 tsp fresh ginger, grated
1 Tbsp onion, chopped

DIRECTIONS

1) Marinate 6 to 8 pieces of chicken for several hours or overnight. Turn pieces over once or twice.
2) Bake at 400°F for 1 hour. Baste and turn chicken a couple times. Remove from oven. Almost done. But not quite!

When my siblings and I started making this dish it would turn out okay, but was never quite as good as mom's. When mom looked over the recipe she said, "Well, you have to thicken the sauce." (We always teased her afterwards that she left out that important detail on purpose.)

HERE'S THE REST OF THE RECIPE:

3) Mix 2 Tbsp cornstarch in ½ cup water.
4) Gradually add ½ cup of juice from chicken. Stir.
5) Gradually pour back into chicken dish. Return to oven for 20 to 30 more minutes.

The chicken should be quite dark and the sauce thick and yummy! Delicious with rice, salad and steamed or roasted vegetables.

FILIPINO ADOBO CHICKEN

Contributed by: Chanel Mandap

Filipino Adobo Chicken—chicken braised in vinegar, soy sauce, and garlic—is a national favourite of the Philippines. Using everyday ingredients, it's an effortless recipe that creates juicy, tender chicken that's coated in an intoxicatingly sweet and tangy glaze. The simplicity of the dish is what truly makes it great! This savoury chicken dish is one of those meals that always reminds me of home and reminds me of all of the times this delicious meal has brought my family together. It is made to be shared and enjoyed over rice—so dig in together!

Fun twists on this recipe can be made by adding peeled, hardboiled eggs or diced potatoes that can be cooked in the sauce. These act as bite-sized flavour bombs!

INGREDIENTS

CHICKEN & MARINADE:

2 lb skin-on, bone-in chicken (thighs or cut, whole chicken)

3 garlic cloves, minced

½ cup soy sauce

⅔ cup white vinegar

4 fresh bay leaves (3 if dried)

FOR COOKING:

2 Tbsp cooking oil, separated

3 garlic cloves, minced

1 small, brown onion, diced

1 ½ cups water

2 Tbsp brown sugar

1 tsp whole black peppercorns (or 2 Tbsp cracked black pepper)

FOR SERVING:

2 green onions, sliced for garnish

Steamed rice

DIRECTIONS

1) Combine chicken and marinade ingredients in a bowl. Marinate for at least 20 minutes or overnight. Note: the longer the time, the better.

2) Heat 1 Tbsp oil in a skillet over high heat. Remove chicken from the marinade (reserve the marinade) and place in a pan. Sear both sides until browned—about 1 minute on each side. Do not cook the chicken all the way through.

3) Remove chicken from the skillet and set aside.

4) Heat the remaining oil in the skillet. Add garlic and onion, cooking for 1 ½ minutes.

5) Add the reserve marinade, water, sugar, and black pepper. Bring it to a simmer then turn down heat to medium high. Simmer 5 minutes.

6) Add chicken. Simmer uncovered for 20–25 minutes (no need to stir), turning chicken at 15 minutes, until the sauce reduces to a thick jam-like syrup.

7) If the sauce isn't thick enough, remove chicken onto a plate and let the sauce simmer by itself—it will thicken much quicker—then return chicken to the skillet to coat in the glaze

8) Coat chicken in the glaze then serve hot over rice. Then share and enjoy!

FRIKADELLER (DANISH MEATBALLS)

Contributed by: Viki Prescott & Kathryn Watts

V iki is a California girl, born in Los Angeles, who travelled in Europe at the age of 17 to join her grandmother. On returning to the U.S. she met Paul, a Danish-Canadian student who would become her husband. They moved back to Canada, married and subsequently had twin daughters in 1970.

Viki's Danish mother-in-law Karen (also living in the Vancouver area at that time) became a huge support and influence in her life and the lives of her daughters. Not least the exposure to Danish cooking and baking.

Frikadeller became one of those often prepared, home cooked meals handed down first to Viki and then to the girls, Tammy and Stacy. Stacy in fact went on to a successful career as a baker and is now part owner in a culinary school in the Vancouver area.

Frikadeller would often be served with red cabbage and boiled potatoes (see Rick Bergh's recipe for red cabbage!).

INGREDIENTS

1 ½ lbs ground beef
½ lb ground pork
1 onion, grated
3–4 slices white bread
⅛ tsp pepper
4 Tbsp flour
½ tsp cloves
1 ½ tsp salt
2 eggs
Milk or Cream

DIRECTIONS

1) Be sure the meat is well ground. Add grated onion and the bread which has been softened in milk. Mix well. Add the remainder of the ingredients. Whites may be used instead of whole eggs. Add the milk or cream a little at a time. Stir well after each addition. Some people use tomato juice instead of milk or cream.

2) Fry the meatballs in a hot pan. Use suet or a good shortening. The meatballs are shaped and placed in the pan with a spoon that has been dipped in the hot fat each time. Fry until lightly brown. Make a gravy to serve with the meatballs by adding more meat juice or bouillon to the pan and thicken with flour which has been added to stock or cream.

HAWAIIAN BEEF

Contributed by: Paul & Frances Beckow

This recipe came with a 'Welcome to the neighbourhood!' casserole over 30 years ago from lovely friends in Kamloops, Dave and Heather. It is from their church cookbook entitled The Church Ladies' Cookbook. Those ladies were really good cooks!

Everyone in the family loved this dish when they didn't agree on too many other meals! You can cook the beef then put it in the slow cooker to simmer all day or you can cook the beef and veggies, add the rest and serve it in half an hour. Paul and I have been retired for eons and don't have to worry about getting a meal on the table PDQ. However, we still love Hawaiian Beef and serve it to our grand girls when they come for dinner.

INGREDIENTS

3 lbs. stewing beef

1 can kidney beans

1 can baked beans in tomato sauce

1 19-oz can pineapple tidbits, with juice

1 onion, chopped

1 cup ketchup

¼ cup brown sugar

1 tsp mustard

1 tsp salt

DIRECTIONS

1) Preheat oven to 350°F if cooking in the oven, or in slow cooker, turn dial to "high."

2) Chop onions and cook in a frying pan on medium until soft.

3) Add beef and cook until browned and there is no pink left in the beef.

4) In a large bowl add the rest of the ingredients and mix well. Pour mixture into a casserole dish or the slow cooker. Add beef and onions.

5) Cook at 350°F for 50–60 minutes. Or in the slow cooker for 4–5 hours.

MARINATED FLANK STEAK

Contributed by: Stephen Lee

When I retired, I promised myself two things: that I would cook more and that I would sing more. I am passionate about both and am fulfilling that promise. Unfortunately, we are not able to host as many dinner parties for our friends and family as we would like, but at least our kids are still able to benefit from our cooking!

This flank steak is our go-to beef/steak dinner as everyone likes it and it serves more people and less expensively than having individual steaks.

This is a simple and relatively inexpensive way of serving beef. It involves a teriyaki-style marinade. Serves 6.

INGREDIENTS

1 flank steak (about 2 lbs.)
2 Tbsp brown sugar
¼ cup light soy
¼ cup Chinese cooking wine (or sherry, or gin)
5 slices ginger
3 cloves garlic, minced

DIRECTIONS

1) Place the steak in a 9-inch casserole dish or any sided dish that can accommodate the steak.
2) Mix the other ingredients in a bowl/measuring cup. Taste and adjust according to taste—saltier (more soy), less salty (more wine), or sweeter (more sugar).
3) Pour marinade over the steak and let it sit in the fridge for at least a couple of hours. Turn the steak over every half hour. Remove from the fridge about an hour before cooking so the meat comes to room temperature.
4) Grill over high heat to desired doneness—about 3 min. per side for medium rare in the thickest part. Steak can also be cooked under broiler.
5) To serve, let cooked steak rest on a platter for about 15 min. then slice against the grain. Be sure to save any drippings to serve with the meat.

MOUSSAKA

Contributed by: Niki Sacoutis and Pantelis Sakoutis

This special moussaka comes from my daddy, Pantelis Sakoutis. He was born on the Greek island of Ikaria where the mythical Icarus would have fallen in the Mediterranean after flying too close to the sun with wax wings. Ikaria is also considered one of the Blue Zones, where people often live well past 100.

Pantelis, a pacifist, was a cook on Greek ships travelling the world in the early 1900s. He had deserted the Greek army. Being philosophical of mind, and adventurous of spirit, he came to Canada where he opened restaurants in Montreal and Ottawa. It is there that he met my French-Canadian mother, Yvette, who was 25 years his junior. They made beautiful moussaka together as well as 4 children. I am the eldest, the keeper of the secret moussaka recipe and now it's yours.

You'll notice the different spellings of our family name. It's not a typo. The real name is Sakoutis, with a "k" as there is no "c" in Greek. When my dad came to Canada, the official who welcomed him spelt his name with a "c" instead of a "k". So we have always been Sacoutis, but out of respect for my dad and our Greek heritage, we spell dad's name Sakoutis.

INGREDIENTS

VEGETABLES:

2 eggplants

4 small zucchinis

4 medium potatoes

Olive oil

MEAT SAUCE:

4 Tbsp olive oil

1 ½ pounds ground beef or lamb

2 onions, chopped

2 garlic cloves, minced

1 796-mL can of tomatoes

½ cup red wine

¼ cup parsley

1 tsp cinnamon

1 tsp oregano

Salt and pepper to taste

CREAM SAUCE:

6 Tbsp butter

¾ cup flour

4 cups hot milk

5 eggs

1 cup parmesan or kefalotyri grated cheese

Salt, pepper and a dash of nutmeg

Cream sauce

DIRECTIONS

1) Slice vegetables lengthwise, 1 cm thick, brush both sides with olive oil. BBQ or broil until lightly done on both sides. Set aside.

2) In a deep frying pan, sauté meat and onions in olive oil until brown. Add tomatoes, parsley, wine, salt, pepper and spices. Simmer until juices thicken.

3) In a large saucepan melt 6 Tbsp butter. Add flour and stir until well blended and golden. Gradually add hot milk, cook and stir until smooth and thickened. (I sometimes make the cream sauce in the microwave). Add salt, pepper and a pinch of nutmeg. In a mixing bowl, beat eggs then add 1 cup of the hot cream sauce and stir until well blended. Slowly stir the egg mixture into the remaining cream sauce. Remove from heat.

ASSEMBLY:

1) Sprinkle bottom of a 9" × 13" baking dish with ¼ cup breadcrumbs.

2) Alternate layers of vegetables (starting with the potatoes) and meat sauce sprinkling each layer with cheese. Finish with a layer of eggplant on top.

3) Pour a little more than ½ of the cream sauce over the vegetables and bake at 350°F for 10 minutes.

4) Meanwhile, return remaining sauce to very low heat and cook stirring occasionally.

5) Pour onto casserole and sprinkle with remaining cheese and continue to bake 45–50 minutes until golden brown.

ROASTED CHICKEN THIGHS WITH DRIED FRUIT

Contributed by: Stephen Lee

When I retired, I promised myself two things: that I would cook more and that I would sing more. I am passionate about both and am fulfilling that promise. Unfortunately, we are not able to host as many dinner parties for our friends and family as we would like, but at least our kids are still able to benefit from our cooking!

This chicken dish is my personal take on the classic Chicken Marbella. It is very simple to make and blends sweet and savoury flavours nicely. I use thighs rather than breasts as they are more moist. Depending on whether you prefer it sweeter or saltier you can adjust the amount of fruit and olives to taste. Serves 6.

INGREDIENTS

1 kg. boneless, skinless chicken thighs, extra
    fat removed*
2 Tbsp brown sugar
¼ cup apple juice
1 Tbsp capers
¼ cup dried apricots
¼ cup dried prunes
12 green olives
12 kalamati olives (nice and salty!)
2 Tbsp red wine vinegar
1 Tbsp chopped fresh oregano
Salt and freshly ground pepper, to taste

* If you prefer thighs with skin and bones, then towards the end of the cooking time you can crisp up the skin under the broiler for about 5 min.

DIRECTIONS

1) Preheat oven to 375°F.
2) Lay dried fruits on bottom of a casserole dish or large deep-sided baking pan and top with remaining ingredients.
3) Bake in oven 45 minutes and serve. (About halfway through, turn the thighs over to ensure even cooking and maintain moisture. If any of the fruit are on top, push them back down as they may burn.)

Pairs with Chenin Blanc or Chardonnay.

SPANIKOPITA

Contributed by: Janet & Gary Dillabaugh

Spanikopita is a savoury Greek dish that translated means "spinach pie." My twin sister, Jean, gave this recipe to me years ago. It was a favourite at the clinic where she worked as an x-ray technician. She used to bring it in for potlucks and events at work. They loved it. So does our family.

INGREDIENTS

20 sheets of filo pastry (one package)
1 cup melted butter (I use olive oil and only as much
    as I need to baste the filo sheets here and there)
3 lbs fresh spinach or 4 frozen packages
2 bunches leeks or 2 large onions
Garlic, mint or dill (optional)
6 eggs
300 mL half-and-half light cream
1 lb crumbled feta (500 grams)
Pinch of nutmeg

DIRECTIONS

1) Thaw spinach, if frozen. Drain spinach in colander and squeeze out excess water. Pan fry onions/leeks in a little olive oil or butter till soft. Add garlic or dill etc.

2) Have filo pastry on counter to thaw and lay out in large sheets.

3) Beat eggs, cream and cheese in a bowl. Fold in onions, spices and spinach, salt, pepper and nutmeg. Set aside.

4) In large 9" × 13" baking dish (or lasagne pan), baste inside with pastry brush and olive oil. Carefully lay one sheet of filo at a time into the dish and baste so the next sheet adheres to the previous one. This can be a little fiddly. If it tears a little here and there do not worry—just do the best you can.

5) When you have 10 sheets down, then take the spinach mixture and add into the dish.

6) Now continue to add the remaining 10 sheets of filo, basting after each layer. When finished, take kitchen sheers and trim the edges so it is flush with the top of the dish.

7) Bake in oven at 375°F for 45 to 55 minutes or until golden brown. Serve with tossed salad.

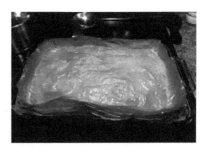

TOAD IN THE HOLE

Contributed by: Judith Daniel

In Great Britain during days of hardship and food shortages, wives and mothers would cook their measly greasy roasts to extract what fat they could, then pour Yorkshire pudding batter around what was left. When ready, this smoking hot pan of goodness would be placed in front of the famished horde where they would tear off chunks of the crunchy brown top to get to the fat-soaked, slightly stodgy, flavourful middle. Everyone filled up on this tasty hot bread before the meagre roast was divided between the children and adults, then served with what few vegetables were available, if any. Over the years the little greasy roasts disappeared and it is now made with sausages. This easy dish has been a mainstay in my family since I was a child, then as a mother, and now it is a regular meal made for and by my grandchildren.

INGREDIENTS

YORKSHIRE PUDDING:

1 cup flour

1 cup milk

4 eggs

½–1 tsp salt

Sausages (any kind of raw sausage – 8 breakfast or 4 dinner)

Fat or oil (if required)

DIRECTIONS

1) Preheat the oven to 450°F.

2) With a whisk, mix the flour, milk, eggs and salt in a bowl but leave it slightly lumpy. Let it sit while the sausages cook. Yorkshire pudding batter gets better over time, so don't be afraid to mix it up a few hours before you want to bake it.

3) Fry, but not fully cook, the sausage. I like to fry the sausages in a cast iron frying pan which can be moved directly into the 450°F oven. If you are using a baking dish, let it heat in the oven so it is as hot as the oven when you place the sausages in the bottom.

4) Once the sausages are partially cooked put them in the baking dish (or leave them in the pan) and pour the Yorkshire Pudding batter over the sausages. Ensure there is a layer of fat or oil in the bottom of the pan to prevent the pudding from sticking. Place in the oven for 45–60 minutes or until done. It will deflate when it comes out unless you cook it to a crunch, so make sure everyone gets a peek before it comes out of the oven!

TOFU IN GARLIC CHILI SAUCE

Contributed by: Janet & Gary Dillabaugh

Gary and I are trying to eat a healthy, more plant-based diet. We are trying to stop the progress of the dementia and better still reverse it. I chose this recipe because I did not know how to cook tofu well. It is usually added to stir fry or similar as it takes on the flavours of the main dish so this tofu was delicious on its own and is also a healthy, tasty alternative to meat, chicken or fish.

INGREDIENTS

Extra firm tofu

2 Tbsp corn starch

¼ cup low sodium soy sauce (I just use wheat free tamari)

2 Tbsp water

2 tsp honey

1 ½ tsp chili garlic sauce

½ tsp rice wine vinegar

2 tsp cornstarch

DIRECTIONS

1) The secret here is in how you prepare the tofu. Choose EXTRA FIRM organic, Non-GMO. Take it out of the packet, usually it's in water, and place on cutting board between two paper towels folded up, two on the bottom and two on the top. Place something heavy on top, a cast iron pan or heavy dish etc. Let sit for 30 minutes. Change paper towels at 15 minutes. Take the tofu and cut into small cubes. Put into large bowl and dust with cornstarch. Use your fingers and toss to make sure all squares covered.

2) Mix all the remaining sauce ingredients in small bowl. Set aside.

3) Heat a frying pan with approximately 1 Tbsp sesame oil (I use avocado oil as it can be heated to a high temperature safely). When pan is hot, toss in the tofu. When brown on the one side, toss to brown all sides of cubes. Don't toss too frequently, to allow to brown and crisp up.

4) When nicely browned toss in the sauce mixture for a minute. Put in serving dish and enjoy. Keep warm in oven or serve immediately.

This recipe is paired with the Cauliflower Rice & Petit Pan Squash, a side dish in this cookbook.

TOURTIÈRE (QUÉBECOIS MEAT PIE)

Contributed by: Edith Phare

The late Mme. Duhamel, in an address to a women's group in Beloeil, QC (ca. 1950), told of her family's traditional tourtière. In the late fall, papa and the boys went out for turtle doves, which she made up into tourtières and partially cooked. She then froze them and left them out on the back stoop. On Christmas Eve, while the family was at midnight mass, Maman would pop the frozen tourtières into a 400°F oven. When mass was over, this was their Christmas dinner at 2 am. A turtle dove in French is a "tourterelle," so at one time a tourtière was not a meat pie but a turtle dove pie, or even a pie made from the now-extinct passenger pigeon.

It became a tradition in our family for my mom (Edith Phare) to make tourtières for our family supper on December 24 each year. It was served with either ketchup or any type of chutney or salsa.

INGREDIENTS

½ lb. lean ground pork
½ lb. ground beef (and/or veal)
1 onion, chopped
½ tsp salt
1 ½ tsp savoury*
¼ tsp pepper
¼ tsp ground cloves*
1 cup hot water
¾ cup breadcrumbs
2 ready-made deep-dish pastry shells (8" or 9")

* Season to your own taste, using more or less savoury and cloves. These amounts of spice are for the "average" taste bud. I usually had my husband, Rowlie, check the seasoning before adding the meat mixture to the pastry-lined pie plate—then I usually end up adding 2–3 times the amount of seasoning! The choice is yours. Bon appétit!

DIRECTIONS

1) Mix first 8 ingredients together and bring to a boil. Simmer for about 20 minutes. Add breadcrumbs and simmer for another 20 minutes.

2) Put into 8" or 9" pie plate, lined with pastry and cover with pastry. At this point, you can freeze it, covering it with tin foil for later use OR if you want to eat it right away, bake it for 15–20 minutes at 425°F until the crust is golden then at 350°F for about 20–25 minutes. If you freeze it, when it comes time to bake it, keep the aluminum foil in place, bake for 1 hour at 350°F, then at 425°F uncovered, until crust is golden.

WHITE CUT VELVET CHICKEN

Contributed by: Stephen Lee

When I retired, I promised myself two things: that I would cook more and that I would sing more. I am passionate about both and am fulfilling that promise. Unfortunately, we are not able to host as many dinner parties for our friends and family as we would like, but at least our kids are still able to benefit from our cooking!

This chicken recipe is something that my family would have regularly, especially for special occasions. It was usually served Chinese-style, with the head and feet attached. The dish was always served with the head pointing toward the guest of honour.

INGREDIENTS

Young chicken/roaster*

Water (enough to cover chicken)

4–5 slices ginger root

3–4 green onions, cut into 3-inch lengths (white part and green)

1 Tbsp (unsalted) rice wine (sake) OR sherry OR gin

1 Tbsp of light soy sauce

* If desired, chicken breasts with skin and bones may be used instead of a whole chicken.

DIRECTIONS

1) Add ginger, green onions, rice wine, and soy sauce to water in a stock pot and bring to a boil.

2) Immerse chicken or, if not enough water, roll chicken in the water to coat the skin and leave breast side down. Bring water back to a rolling boil.

3) Cover pot. Turn heat to low and leave covered for half an hour.

4) Lift chicken out and drain it. Refrigerate on a plate overnight. Strain ginger and green onion from pot and use as soup base.

5) Cut the cold chicken into bite-size pieces, meat and bone, with a cleaver or strip off the breast meat (with or without skin) and then cut into bite size pieces.

6) For a dip, mince equal amounts of ginger and green onions and put into a heat-proof dish. For two tablespoons of the mixture add enough salt to cover the top, about ¾ Tbsp. Heat 3 Tbsp of oil until very hot and then pour over the mixture. Let cool. Oyster sauce can also be used as a dip.

7) Pieces of fresh cilantro may be served along with the chicken.

CAULIFLOWER RICE & PETIT PAN SQUASH

Contributed by: Janet & Gary Dillabaugh

PETIT PAN SQUASH INGREDIENTS

1 squash
Olive oil or butter
Garlic (optional)
Honey (optional)

DIRECTIONS

Also very easy. I like to half or quarter the squash depending on the size of them. You can fry in a little olive oil or butter. You can add garlic if you wish. I like to add a little honey and caramelize them. Pan fry till nicely browned.

Gary and I are trying to eat a healthy, more plant-based diet. We are trying to stop the progress of the dementia and better still reverse it. These healthy sides go really well with the Tofu in Garlic Chili Sauce, one of the main dishes in this cookbook.

CAULIFLOWER RICE INGREDIENTS

1 head cauliflower
Olive oil or butter
Salt and pepper

DIRECTIONS

I love this dish. It is so easy and healthy and a good substitute for rice or potatoes and you get your veggies. Break cauliflower up into segments and put into food processor or blender. Pulse for a few seconds till small and crumbly. Toss in frypan with olive oil or butter, salt and pepper for 3—5 minutes. Serve hot. This is the easiest and quickest dish you will make. You can experiment with favorite herbs, but we like it just as it is.

BENGALI GREEN PEPPER AALOOR DOM

Contributed by: Sirima Sengupta

Aaloo (pronounced Aa-loo in Bengali) means "potato." Dom (pronounced in Bengali almost like Tom but with a D) is a way of slow-cooking food. Aaloor (or Aaloo-r) means "of potato." Aaloo Dom is made innumerable ways in India. This recipe has a special twist to the Bengali Aaloor Dom (from the Eastern part of India), which is traditionally a lightly spiced potato in a sauce made with onions, tomato and spices. The twist of adding green peppers to Aaloor Dom is something unique to my family and reminds me of my family back in India.

I wanted to share this recipe as it is simple, easy to prepare and tastes delicious. It goes very well with any form of bread and can be eaten any time of the day—for breakfast, lunch or supper. It can be prepared less spicy and still tastes great, plus it is a vegan recipe.

This is a lightly spiced potato dish with onion and green pepper sauce.

MAIN INGREDIENTS

200 g baby potatoes
2 Tbsp oil
1 tsp cumin seeds
1 ½ tsp coriander powder
½ tsp turmeric powder
¼ tsp Kashmiri red chili powder
    (optional—very hot)
Fresh coriander leaves (for garnish)

INGREDIENTS FOR THE GRAVY/SAUCE

1 ½ Tbsp oil
1 cup green pepper, chopped
½ cup onion, chopped
1-inch cube ginger, chopped
½ tsp black pepper powder
Salt to taste

DIRECTIONS

SAUCE:

1) Heat oil in a pan. Add onion, ginger and green pepper. Stir and fry until onions are slightly browned. Add salt and black pepper and cook for 3 more minutes. Set aside to cool.

2) Once mixture is room temperature, purée in blender. The sauce is complete.

POTATO MIXTURE:

1) Boil water in a medium-sized pot. Add baby potatoes (if you don't have baby potatoes, you can use regular potatoes cut into pieces).

2) Cook until softened but not mushy. Drain the water and peel the skin from the potatoes. Set aside.

3) Heat oil in a second pan (or reuse the pan in which the ingredients for the sauce was cooked).

4) Add the cumin seeds and let them crackle for a few seconds. Once the cumin seeds start turning brown, add the boiled potatoes.

5) Fry potatoes for a few minutes, stirring occasionally. Once the potatoes are slightly browned, add coriander, turmeric, red chili powder (optional) and salt.

6) Cook until oil starts to separate from the sides, then add onion and green pepper sauce. Cook for 5–7 minutes on low heat.

7) Add ½ cup water and cook on low heat for another 5–7 minutes.

8) Garnish with fresh coriander. Serve hot.

DANISH RED CABBAGE

Contributed by: Rick Bergh

Eating boiled red cabbage…I would have put that in the same category as having a root canal.

Or so I thought…

I remember the exact date I had red cabbage for the first time. I was dating my first wife, Pam. She had invited me to spend Christmas dinner at her home and with her family.

Pam had both Finnish and Danish backgrounds. I discovered that red cabbage was a mainstay for Danish families when they were celebrating. It was usually paired with turkey.

Let me set the scene for you. This was my first Christmas with Pam's family and only the second time I'd met her parents. I wanted to make a good impression.

After some casual conversation, we were invited into the formal dining room. It was beautifully decorated for Christmas. The table was set with fine china and linen napkins. The food was on the table in covered porcelain bowls. Mmmm—lots of wonderful smells…but wait, "What's that smell?" I asked myself. It wasn't all that pleasant—it smelt sour. As soon as the lids were removed, the smell became all the more pungent. I looked and saw where the odour was coming from—red cabbage. Yuck!

What was I to do? I could not refuse a food item. I didn't want to appear to be a picky eater. I was there to impress, remember? Nor did I want to simply take a "no-thank-you" helping—that would also have said something. So I put a big portion on my plate (and held my breath).

I started by eating what I liked first: turkey, gravy, mashed potatoes, stuffing, peas, carrots. But then I knew I would eventually have to face eating the red cabbage. So I put a fork-load into my mouth and had a glass of juice at the ready as a chaser. And to my surprise, I LOVED it!

The next day, that red cabbage tasted even better! We had turkey sandwiches topped with red cabbage and it was delicious!

Now every time we gather together as family and have turkey, red cabbage is part of the menu. And when I eat that red cabbage, it reminds me of Pam, who died at age 47 but is still an important part of our family.

INGREDIENTS

1 head purple cabbage (chopped)

2–3 cups white vinegar

Water—enough to cover ¾ of the cabbage after adding the vinegar

4 apples, peeled and chopped

½ cup brown sugar

3 Tbsp butter (or lard)

1 cup real bacon bits

DIRECTIONS

1) Mix ingredients in a slow cooker.

2) Cook on LOW for a minimum of 10 hours.

POTATO KUGEL

Contributed by: Susan-Rose Slatkoff & Bram Goldwater

Kugel is a Jewish dish that is best described as baked pudding. Originating in Germany over 800 years ago, it was popular throughout Eastern Europe. There are actually many different types of kugel—noodle, sweet, savoury—but potato kugel is usually served during Passover and is often accompanied by other holiday classics like matzo ball soup, brisket and roasted chicken. But it tastes good any time of the year!

Potato Kugel can be addictive and is even good cold. I often hear leftovers calling me from the fridge at night. Enjoy—and nosh to your heart's content.

Serves about 4 people, depending on how many kugel lovers are around.

INGREDIENTS

5 large potatoes (we use russets)

3 eggs

¼ cup matzoh meal (if unavailable, you can use flour—but matzoh meal is best. You can get it at Aubergine on Gladstone near the Belfry—if you live in Victoria, BC)

1 grated medium onion

½ cup oil

1 tsp salt

¼ tsp pepper

DIRECTIONS

1) Preheat oven to 400°F.

2) Grease a baking pan with the oil and leave the rest in the baking pan—heat in the oven.

3) Half fill a large bowl with water. Grate potatoes on a fine grater directly into the water (keeps potatoes from turning brown). Drain off most of the water (leave a little bit to create steam and moisten kugel).

4) Add grated onion, eggs, matzoh meal, salt and pepper and pour heated oil in kugel (be careful). Mix well.

5) Put mixture into greased pan and bake for about an hour or until a brown crust has formed on top.

PROVENÇAL VEGETABLE TIAN

Contributed by: Dinah & Barry Ellett

The story is short and sweet, as this was a new recipe for us.

We had a busy weekend with two sets of guests coming for BBQ's, two days apart. The first couple enjoyed this vegetable dish with BBQ Loin Lamb Chops, and the second couple had it with BBQ Strip Loin Steak, medium rare, cut in fairly thick slices. It was also served with new potatoes, sprinkled with cilantro and fresh green beans from Sun Wings on Oldfield Road (Victoria, BC).

The second day we put one row of the vegetables in a Pyrex meat loaf dish and reheated it at 350°F for about 15 minutes. It would take a good 20 minutes if straight from the fridge.

INSTRUCTIONS

4 medium vine tomatoes
1 large yellow zucchini
1 large green zucchini
1 large yellow onion
5 or 6 garlic cloves finely sliced
A few sprigs of thyme and rosemary
Either chili flakes, or smoked paprika and pepper
    flakes (use carefully)
Fresh basil

DIRECTIONS

1) Preheat oven to 350°F.
2) Sauté the onion in olive oil until soft adding the garlic cloves halfway through. Add the thyme and chili seasoning. Cook another minute and then place in the bottom of a lightly oiled casserole baking dish. I also used a little sugar on the tomatoes before placing them in the baking dish. This takes the acid out of them.
3) Cut the zucchini and tomatoes in ¼-inch slices and place on edge in the baking dish, alternating vegetables and making sure they fit fairly snugly together.
4) Generously salt and pepper, place a few more sprigs of thyme and rosemary on top and drizzle with olive oil.
5) Bake for 45 to 60 minutes until tender and juicy. Serve with fresh basil on top.

Note: I basted the vegetables with the onion mixture after 45 minutes of cooking to get a better flavour, then continued to bake for another 15 minutes.

In his younger years, Al was always very involved in sports, either as coach of our kids' sports or as a player on a variety of baseball leagues in the city. Mainly through the 70's, 80's and 90's and well into the 2000's. There were always team barbeques and parties. The only dish I was allowed to bring to these events were Schwartz's! When word was sent out of a party, it would be requested that I bring my famous Schwartz's! The same request was made for our yearly family reunion at Thanksgiving which has been happening for the last forty-two years. This dish is a highlight at any event!

INGREDIENTS

1 kg bag of hash browns

500 g sour cream

1 medium/large grated onion

2 tins cream mushroom soup

2+ cups grated cheddar cheese

Parmesan cheese

¼ cup melted butter

DIRECTIONS

1) Mix first 5 ingredients together in a very large bowl and then put in a 9" × 13" pan.

2) Sprinkle with parmesan and melted butter over top.

3) Bake at 400°F for 45 minutes.

CHILI SAUCE

Contributed by: Deborah Austin

I thought a photo of my Mum, Muriel, would be more appropriate than one of me, as it is her recipe from the 40's.

Mum's generation went through the depression and WW2 and therefore learned to economize in every way possible.

Whenever I make this chili sauce, I always double the recipe because our sons' families wanted several jars. I prefer to use the small mason jars.

I hope you enjoy your chili sauce.

This recipe is a cross between Salsa and Chutney.

INGREDIENTS

6-quart basket of ripe tomatoes—peeled and cut into small pieces (approx. 30 average sized tomatoes)

6 cups celery diced finely

4 cups onion diced finely

⅛ cup mustard seed

2 medium green peppers, seeded and chopped finely

½ cup pickling salt

6 cups sugar

2 cups cider vinegar

⅛ tsp cayenne pepper

DIRECTIONS

1) Put all the veggies in a large container and sprinkle with the pickling salt. Mix well and let stand overnight. Drain through a colander and discard liquid.

2) Put pulp in large kettle and add remaining ingredients. Bring to a boil. Stir often to prevent scorching. Let mixture boil at full boil uncovered until it looks thick enough...similar to salsa.

3) Put into sterilized mason jars and seal immediately or put in canning kettle and seal in hot/boiling bath.

4) I prefer the smaller size mason jars. Makes approximately 6 quarts.

I use this chili sauce on chicken dishes, with eggs and bacon for breakfast, with Mac and Cheese....and many other applications. ENJOY!

BOTERKOEK

Contributed by: Jean Carlson

INGREDIENTS

⅔ cup butter
1 cup sugar
1 ½ tsp almond extract
1 egg
1½ cups flour*
½ tsp baking powder
Slivered almonds

This recipe works equally well with gluten-free flour, which makes it a favourite for a large group.

This is a heavy Dutch butter cake, originating from the Netherlands. A very good friend gave me the recipe when we were first married, and it has always been a family favourite ever since. We always refer to it as "Almond Ring." For our daughter's wedding we made twelve dozen individual cakes in muffin tins and that worked really well. We had an individual cake at each place setting with a note explaining that, instead of favors, we would donate $5 for each guest to be divided between the Alzheimer and Parkinson societies in honor of the grandparents.

I usually double the recipe and make two. It freezes well.

Enjoy!

DIRECTIONS

1) Line the bottom of a round 8-inch cake pan with parchment paper.
2) Cream butter, sugar and almond extract. Whisk the egg with a fork and add all except 1 tsp. Add the flour and baking powder. Press the soft dough into the prepared pan.
3) Glaze the top with the teaspoon of egg and cover with slivered almonds.
4) Bake at 350°F for 25–30 minutes or until golden brown.

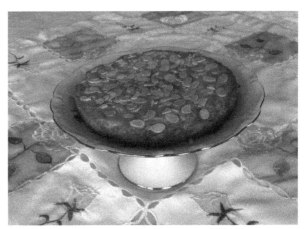

BUTTER HORNS

Contributed by: Connie Bergeron

This recipe was written out by my daughter, Mailyn, and then decorated by my granddaughter, Willow. This has been a family favourite for years, so much so that I had a hard time making them and keeping enough in the freezer for Christmas morning!

Butter Horns

- 1 cup butter
- dash of salt
- 3 cups flour
- 18 oz. (500gr.) container of cottage cheese.

- Mix all ingredients well & refrigerate overnight.
- Divide dough into 3 equal parts.
- Roll each part into a circle, then cut into pie shapes (usually 12 wedges). Roll each wedge starting at large end & ending with the point on top.
- Bake at 350° for 30-40 mins.
- Top with following icing:
- After butter horns are iced, sprinkle with some slivered almonds.

- 3 tbsp cream/milk
- 3/4 c icing sugar
- 2 dashes almond flavouring.

"This has been a family favourite for years, so much so that I had a hard time making & keeping enough in the freezer for christmas morning!" —Connie

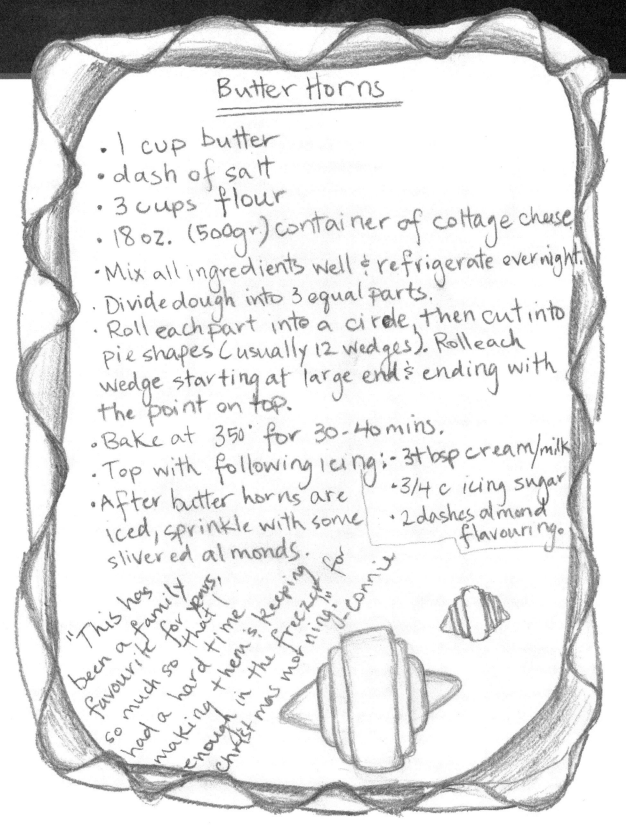

CAMPING CAKE

Contributed by: Sheila & William Bill

This is a well-travelled cake. It has been "camping" from the west coast of Vancouver Island to the Saskatchewan prairies and many places in between. It has been up hill and down dale in backpacks, kayaks and bicycle bags. Our grandchildren gave it the name Camping Cake; no camping without the cake! I think it was the lure of the chocolate chips.

INGREDIENTS

1 cup soft butter
2 cups sugar
3 eggs
⅔ cup plain yogurt
1 tsp vanilla extract
2¼ cups sifted all-purpose flour
½ tsp baking soda
½ tsp salt
1 tsp ground mace
½ tsp ground allspice
½ tsp cinnamon
¼ tsp ground cloves
The Secret ingredient:
    chocolate chips, as many as you like.
Icing sugar

DIRECTIONS

1) Heat oven to 325°F. Grease and flour a 10-inch bundt or angel food pan.
2) Beat butter at medium speed on mixer until fluffy. Beat in sugar gradually. Add eggs one at a time and beat well after each addition. Stir in yogurt and vanilla.
3) Sift flour, soda, salt and spices together and stir into first mixture. Beat at medium speed for 4 minutes, scraping sides and bottom of bowl often. Fold in chocolate chips with a rubber spatula.
4) Turn into prepared pan and bake until a toothpick stuck in centre comes out clean, about 1 hour and 10 minutes. Cool 10 minutes in pan then turn out on rack. When cool put on serving plate and sift icing sugar over top.

Enjoy with a glass of milk or a cup of tea.

CHOCOLATE CHIP SQUARES

Contributed by: Margie & Brian Noonan

These squares are a family favourite at Christmas. They are faster and easier than cookies!

INGREDIENTS

1 cup flour
½ tsp baking powder
¼ tsp salt
⅛ tsp baking soda
⅓ cup butter
1 cup brown sugar
1 egg
1 tsp vanilla
1 package Chipits
½ cup chopped nuts (if desired)

DIRECTIONS

1) Mix well and smooth into a small square baking pan.
2) Bake at 350°F for 25 minutes.

WHIPPED SHORTBREAD

Contributed by: Margie & Brian Noonan

In our earlier days of family life, I used to love baking at Christmas. My mother made about 5 things that I just loved and would make each year. But as the years passed and my life became busier with four children, Brian, and full-time teaching, I found that I baked less and less!

But a favourite of our family was Whipped Shortbread! It was fairly quick and easy and became the Christmas cookie treat.

INGREDIENTS

1 cup butter (soft)

1 ½ cups flour

½ cup icing sugar

DIRECTIONS

1) Mix and then beat slowly with a mix-master for about 10 minutes.

2) Drop spoonfuls onto a lightly greased (or non-stick) cookie sheet.

3) Bake at 350°F for about 17 minutes. Can be kept in freezer.

GARRY'S SPECIAL DESSERT PANCAKES

Contributed by: Garry & Adele Wickett

This is the recipe that our kids loved growing up and which our grandchildren always wanted when they stayed overnight. I guess it also meant a relaxed breakfast rather than the usual hurried "eat and run" variety, so we would sit around, talk and visit as we ate.

Recently our daughter, Mim, befriended a group of refugees/asylum-seekers from Afghanistan and Kurdish families, all of whom fled dangers to their lives. They are all from backgrounds that do not eat pork. So Mim asked me for the pancake recipe since it's easy and quick to prepare in her busy life and poses no dietary issues (she, on the other hand, is given all kinds of delicious dishes which are showered upon her as a "thank you" for her care and friendship—they call their "angel").

I don't really remember where this recipe came from, but Adele's handwritten recipe card says on it Garry's Special Dessert Pancakes. They were usually served with Roger's Golden Syrup but sometimes with yogurt and fresh fruit.

INGREDIENTS

¾ cup flour

¼ cup corn starch

1 egg

1 ¼ cup milk

Pinch of salt

1 Tbsp vegetable oil

DIRECTIONS

1) Mix flour and cornstarch together. Make a well in the center, add egg, gradually beat in milk until smooth.

2) Heat oil in the frying pan so water droplets dance in the pan when at the best temperature.

3) Pour pancake-sized batter in greased pan (it will spread out quite thinly, so don't pour out too much at a time).

4) Cook until the top bubbles and loses its wet sheen (about 2 min), then flip over and brown on the other side (about 1 min).

5) Top with syrup, fresh fruit and yogurt.

GINGER SNAP COOKIES

Contributed by: Pam DeMontigny

My granddaughter, Grace, and I are using a hand-written and much-smudged recipe for ginger snap cookies from my mom. My son, Dustin, walked by as we were mixing them and commented, "You know what grandma always said...those smudges are a sign that the recipe was well used, so it must be a good recipe." I'll say. My mom used to bring these cookies every summer to the lake for DECADES.

INGREDIENTS

¾ cup softened butter

½ cup sugar

2 beaten eggs

½ cup molasses

2 tsp vinegar

3 cups flour

1 ½ tsp soda

2 tsp ginger

1 tsp cinnamon

½ tsp cloves and nutmeg

DIRECTIONS

1) Cream butter and sugar. Add the eggs, molasses and vinegar and mix. Mix dry ingredients together and then add to the wet. Mix. Put in fridge to chill. When ready to bake, roll into small balls. Dunk into a bowl of sugar. Place on cookie sheet and flatten.

2) Bake at 350°F for 10 to 12 minutes.

GRANNY FOSTER'S MINCEMEAT COOKIES

Contributed by: Andrea Warner

My family is of British descent and mincemeat is a must at Christmas time. As she was of the 'waste not, want not' era, I think my Granny's mincemeat cookies began as a way of using up leftover mincemeat in January. For me, eating these mincemeat cookies brings back the comfort that comes from visiting beloved grandparents. I tried to get the recipe from Granny, but it came in the form of 'some of this, and then some of that…'! I have adapted the following recipe so that it tastes similar to my grandmother's cookies, which had a good proportion of mincemeat… but I added some oatmeal and nuts to make them a bit healthier. I hope you enjoy them…you don't need to wait until January to make them!

INGREDIENTS

½ cup shortening

½ cup sugar

1 egg

1 cup mincemeat

1 ⅓ cups flour

⅔ cup oatmeal

½ tsp baking soda

½ tsp salt

½ cup chopped pecans/walnuts

DIRECTIONS

1) Preheat oven to 350°F and lightly grease cookie sheets.
2) Cream shortening and sugar until light and fluffy; add egg and beat well.
3) Combine flour, soda and salt; mix well, and then stir into shortening/sugar/egg mixture. Add nuts.
4) Drop by teaspoons onto cookie sheets. Bake for 18 to 20 minutes.

Note: you can omit nuts and/or you can just use 2 cups flour instead of the mixture of flour and oatmeal.

ICE BOX CAKE

Contributed by: Pat & Flo Parker

Flo got this recipe from her mother-in-law in about 1950 in Montreal. Even at that time, ice boxes were passé and not in general use. However, they would have been common when Grammie was growing up, and when she got married during the Great Depression. She spoke of making this cake back when she herself had an icebox in her modern kitchen. Margarine was relatively uncommon at this time so butter was used for cooking.

Keep in ice box or new-fangled refrigerator!

INGREDIENTS
½ cup butter
½ cup white sugar
2 Tbsp cocoa
1 egg, well beaten
½ tsp vanilla
¾ cup chopped nuts
About 13 double graham wafers, coarsely broken into ½" pieces

ICING:
1 Tbsp cocoa
Lump (1 Tbsp) of butter
Icing sugar (4 heaping Tbsp)
2 Tbsp boiling water

DIRECTIONS
1) Mix butter, sugar, cocoa, egg and vanilla in a saucepan.
2) Once melted, cook 1 minute more over medium heat, stirring constantly.
3) Remove from stove.
4) Add graham wafer chunks and nuts.
5) Press into an 8" × 8" greased pan.

ICING:
1) Cream cocoa, butter and icing sugar together in a small bowl.
2) Stir in boiling water.
3) Spread mixture in a thin layer over cake.
4) Chill before cutting into squares.
5) Leave the cake in the pan. You could sprinkle icing sugar over the top as an option.

IMPOSSIBLE PIE

Contributed by: Dinah & Barry Ellett

This is a recipe from Mollie, Barry's Mum, who moved to Victoria in 1979, just after we moved here from Toronto. Mollie and Jack decided to come here for a more temperate climate, as they were originally from Winnipeg.

We used to have Sunday dinners together every week, taking turns to cook. Mollie was always very good at making desserts and cookies. Impossible Pie with Coconut was a favourite.

The appeal for me, apart from the taste, was the simplicity to make it. As you will see from the recipe, all the ingredients go into a blender and are mixed for only 30 seconds.

It gets its name, Impossible Pie, by the crust going to the bottom of the pie plate, the custard in the middle, and the crust of coconut and nutmeg forming on the top.

About 10 years ago, I added the berries, either raspberries or strawberries mixed with a little Triple Sec or Strawberry Balsamic Vinegar to go with the pie. Flynn, our grandson, who is now a 5'10" 14-year old, added the "Squirty Cream," as he called it when he was about 10 years old.

And so the family favourite has evolved into the great easy dessert to be had at any occasion.

The photo shows a picture of Mollie at the left-hand side of the pie, with the "Squirty Cream" on the right.

Enjoy and impress your family and friends!!!

INGREDIENTS

4 eggs

¼ cup (½ stick) margarine

2 cups of milk

¾ cup granulated sugar

½ cup Original Pancake Mix

¾ tsp baking powder

⅛ tsp salt

½ cup coconut (optional, although it is best with it)

DIRECTIONS

1) Mix all ingredients in a blender for 30 seconds.

2) Pour into a greased and floured 10-inch pie pan or Pyrex dish.

3) Bake at 350°F for 45 minutes or until brown. I bake it for 50–53 minutes.

4) Nutmeg may be sprinkled on top if desired.

LEMON BUTTER COFFEE CAKE
Contributed by: Debra Sheets

I received this recipe from my mom as part of a favorite family recipes cookbook she put together for me—the cookbook was the best present ever! It had all the special recipes that my mom cooked as I was growing up. My mom always made this delicious coffeecake for holidays—it was a special treat for family gatherings.

The original recipe called for oranges—but she modified it to use lemons which I think gives it a  delicious citrus flavor. It's easy to make and I've continued to make this coffeecake over the years. It reminds me of my mom and what an amazing cook she is! It freezes well, so if your household is small, package it up to enjoy it again at a later time. Enjoy!

INGREDIENTS

1 bag active dry yeast
¼ cup warm water
1 cup sugar
1 tsp salt
2 eggs
½ cup sour cream
7 Tbsp butter, melted (6 + 1 Tbsp)
2 ¾ cups flour
1 cup pecans or walnuts, chopped
2 Tbsp lemon rind, grated

GLAZE:

¾ cup sugar
⅓ cup sour cream
2 Tbsp lemon juice
¼ cup butter

DIRECTIONS

1) Soften yeast in warm water in mixing bowl. Stir in ¼ cup sugar, salt, eggs, sour cream and 6 Tbsp melted butter. Gradually add flour to form a stiff dough, beating well after each addition. For first additions of flour, use mixer on medium speed. Cover, let rise in warm place (85–90 degrees) until light and doubled, about 2 hours. This is a slow-rising dough so it may take longer.

2) Combine ¾ cup sugar, ¾ cup nuts and lemon rind. Knead dough on well-floured surface about 15 times. Roll out ½ of dough to a 12-inch circle. Brush with 1 Tbsp melted butter. Sprinkle with half of sugar-nut mixture. Cut into 12 wedges. Roll up starting with side end and rolling to point. Repeat with remaining dough. Place rolls, point side down in 3 rows on a well-greased 9" × 13" pan. Cover, let rise in warm place until light and doubled, about 1 hour or longer.

3) Bake at 350°F for 25 to 30 minutes until golden brown. Leave in pan, pour hot glaze over hot coffeecake. Sprinkle with remaining nuts. Serve warm or cold.

GLAZE

Combine ingredients in saucepan. Boil 3 minutes stirring constantly.

LEMON FOOL

Contributed by: Dinah & Barry Ellett

This has been a family favourite made by my mother, Dorothy, since I was very young. I believe she told me it was called Fool because it is so easy to make. In other words, anyone of any age can make this scrumptious dessert.

It was usually made for a Sunday dinner, which in England, and many places, is a special meal when everyone gathers together. It is often served with Petit Fours, which are small, sweet bite-sized confectionaries. Since I have lived in Victoria for 41 years, I buy these at the Dutch Bakery on Fort Street.

Enjoy the dessert as well as the simplicity to make it.

INGREDIENTS

1 small tub of whipping cream

1 jar of Lemon Curd from Murchie's (they only have one size). The dessert will not be as good if you use a substitute lemon curd.

DIRECTIONS

1) Whip the cream until it forms peaks in a large bowl. Fold in the Lemon Curd with a large metal spoon until well blended.

2) Make the morning or afternoon before serving. Decorate with a sprig of mint or other green herb.

3) It can also be made with slightly sweetened raspberries in the cream instead of the Lemon Curd.

4) Refrigerate until ready to serve, letting it sit at room temperature for 15 minutes so that the flavour comes through.

RICHELIEU MOULD

Contributed by: Brenda Backus & Mackenzie Backus-Vaughan

Is it dessert or a side dish? I was just watching the news and there was a segment on how the jellied salad is making a comeback and taking Instagram by storm. I grew up on the prairies, and the jellied salad had a place at every big important food gathering. My husband loved the Richelieu Mould I made, and it became a staple at every Christmas and Thanksgiving dinner. As the kids got older, they would roll their eyes and mock the jiggly spectacle. After my husband died, my daughter and daughters-in-law began to take over the chore of big dinner making. Everyone thought something was missing from all the dishes on the table, and shockingly they were missing the Richelieu Mould. That made us all smile, and I had to make it for the next celebration meal.

INGREDIENTS

1 package cherry Jello
1 cup boiling water
1 can pitted cherries
2 Tbsp orange juice
¾ cup diced orange sections
1 cup whipped cream
¼ cup toasted chopped almonds

DIRECTIONS

1) Dissolve Jello powder in water.
2) Drain cherries. Add cold water to cherry syrup to make ¾ cup.
3) Add cherry syrup and orange juice to jelly. Chill until thick.
4) Fold in cherries and oranges.
5) Pour into mould. Chill until thick.
6) Unmould. Garnish with whipped cream and almonds.

Favorite Recipe

Richelieu Mould

1 pkge. cherry jello   2 tbsp. orange juice
1 cup boiling water   3/4 cup diced orange sections
1 can pitted cherries

Dissolve jelly powder in water. Drain cherries.
Add cold water to cherry syrup to make 3/4 cup
Add cherry syrup + orange juice to jelly.
Chill until thick. Fold in cherries + oranges.
Pour into mould. Chill until thick. Unmould.
Garnish with 1 cup whipped cream + 1/4 cup toasted
chopped almonds.

Source _____   Who likes it _____

SUCRE À LA CRÈME

Contributed By: Rollande Précourt

In Québec, le Sucre à la crème is a holiday season tradition as a dessert or an afternoon treat. When I was working at school in Calgary, one of the teachers brought some Sucre à la crème for the staff. As it was an easy microwave recipe everybody wanted to get it. I typed the recipe for everyone, and it was the beginning of my own Sucre à la crème. I started to make it for my family to please my son. Since then we eat Sucre à la crème every holiday season. The story of Sucre à la crème is still alive because my son makes his own Sucre à la crème. He even sells it at the Christmas Market in Nelson, BC, where it is always a success.

INGREDIENTS #1
½ lb butter
3 cups brown sugar
1 cup 35% cream

INGREDIENTS #2
4 cups icing sugar
1 tsp vanilla extract

DIRECTIONS
1) Put #1 ingredients in a large microwave-safe bowl and microwave on high for 6 min. Stir and microwave for another 6 min on high.
2) Add ingredients #2. Use an electric mixer to beat the mixture for 3 minutes.
3) Pour into a non-greased 9" × 13" rectangular glass dish. Refrigerate until firm. Cut into squares when set.
4) Add walnuts if desired.

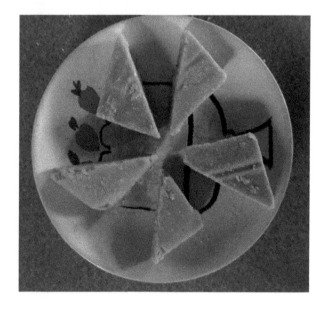

YOGURT CAKE

Contributed by: Niki Sacoutis

My dad, Pantelis, made the moussaka (see page 26). I loved it!

My mom, Yvette, had a very sweet tooth until the day she died at age 88. She really preferred this rather sweet yogurt cake and made it for us (???) quite often. The cake, like most Greek pastry, is moist and, as she said, "Ben Sucré!" I bake the cake when I miss her.

INGREDIENTS

½ cup butter
½ tsp baking soda
1 ½ cups sugar
Pinch of salt
2 eggs
1 cup yogurt
2 ½ cups flour
Syrup: see below

DIRECTIONS

1) Cream butter and sugar together. Beat in eggs. Sift flour, soda and salt together and add to butter mixture alternately with the yogurt. Turn batter in a greased 9" × 13" pan and bake in a 375°F oven for 30–40 minutes or until cake tests done. Remove from oven and pour cool syrup over the hot cake.
2) Yields about 20 pieces.

SYRUP

1) Combine 2 cups of water and 1 cup of sugar. Bring to a boil and boil for 10 minutes. Cool.

RESEARCH

From left to right: Erica Phare-Bergh, Dr. Mary Kennedy, Dr. André Smith, Dr. Debra Sheets, Dr. Stuart MacDonald

I n 2017, Dr. Debra Sheets (Professor of Nursing at the University of Victoria), Dr. Stuart MacDonald (Department of Psychology), Dr. André Smith (Department of Sociology), Dr. Mary Kennedy (Department of Music) received a grant from the Alzheimer Society of Canada and the Pacific Alzheimer Research Foundation to pilot the choir. They secured Erica Phare-Bergh, a professional conductor, to lead the choir as artistic director and within one year established 6 Voices in Motion choirs. These are some of the amazing research results.

FIRST: THE FACTS

Over 1.1 million Canadians are currently affected either directly or indirectly by some form of dementia.

In the United States, 5.8 million people have also been diagnosed with the disease. Many family and friends wonder how best to support their loved one or friend as the disease progresses.

Stigma represents one of the biggest barriers to living with dignity following a dementia diagnosis. According to the Alzheimer Society of Canada, almost half of Canadians would not want others to know if they have dementia for fear of stigmatization — as a consequence, many experience social isolation.

Why is this of concern? Social isolation is linked to elevated stress hormones and inflammation— well-known risk factors for numerous diseases and death. Research findings indicate that social isolation poses a health risk comparable to being sedentary or smoking 15 cigarettes per day. These findings prompted the United Kingdom to appoint a Minister for Loneliness in 2018—a policy initiative worth considering as we implement our own National Dementia Strategy.

SECOND: THE RESEARCH RESULTS

Social singing draws upon emotional and procedural brain systems unaffected by dementia. Those with the disease participate in choir to the same degree as any other individual—a critical consideration for increasing social contact and reducing stigma.

IMPROVEMENT IN EPISODIC MEMORY

Participation in the choir resulted in significant improvement in episodic memory (the recall of details from long-term memory) for both individuals with dementia as well as their family caregivers.

Memories of specific events and experiences are examples of episodic memory. Episodic memories are important because they allow you to recall personal experiences that are an important part of your life. Research findings from Voices in Motion suggest that the benefits of choir (improving quality of life and affect, reducing levels of agitation and distress) result in improved brain function and the corresponding ability to create new memories in spite of dementia.

GAINS IN MEMORY FUNCTION FOR PERSON'S WITH DEMENTIA

Participation in the choir saw modest gains in memory function for PWD, with much larger gains observed for caregivers. Memory Gains is the act of improving one's memory or neuroplasticity.

PRONOUNCED DIFFERENCES IN BRAIN ACTIVATION

Participation in the choir (group singing) in comparison to solo singing resulted in pronounced differences in brain activation:

A. Increased Oxygenation of the frontal cortex of the brain was measured for the solo versus social singing condition. Increased oxygenation/activation was observed while singing alone, which likely reflects both increased novelty as well as stress (as all previous rehearsals required group singing). In contrast, during choral (group) singing, the reduced levels of activation for this same brain region likely reflects reliance on other brain systems (emotional, procedural) to successfully participate in choir. Why do these differences matter? Notably, the frontal cortex is one of the regions of the brain known to deteriorate with dementia; accordingly, devising activities (such as singing well-known songs with a group) that minimize recruitment of such brain regions with enhance successful participation for those with dementia.

B. Social singing elicits neurochemical brain changes that enhance contact, coordination and cooperation with others. Neurochemicals like dopamine, serotonin, and norepinephrine are crucial for mood stabilization. They are not found in the same regions of the brain nor in abundance in the brains of those suffering from depression.

C. Music is a super-stimulus, drawing upon many brain systems unaffected by dementia, that permits those with the disease to participate in choir to the same degree as any other individual (a critical consideration for increasing social contact and reducing stigma).

REDUCED LEVELS OF STRESS, ANXIETY & DEPRESSION

Participation in the choir reduced levels of stress, anxiety and depression for both the person with dementia and their family members—key factors that are known to impair memory function.

Memory is the set of processes used to encode, store, and retrieve information over different periods of time. Among the many subtypes of dementia, memory impairments are most pronounced for those with Alzheimer's Disease due to pronounced changes in a brain region linked to encoding and retrieving memories. Increased stress in general, and caregiver distress in particular, is also known to impair memory function.

The most notable improvements in memory and reductions in depressive symptoms were observed for caregivers—a finding that may reflect the social benefits of the choir intervention (meeting others experiencing similar changes, having a social outlet, overcoming the tendency to withdraw socially).

THIRD: THE INVITATION

To learn more about the research behind Voices in Motion or to request information about starting a Voices in Motion choir community in your community, go to our website, www.voicesinmotionchoirs.org

Visit voicesinmotionchoirs.org to sign up for our Good Vibrations newsletter for information about upcoming events, new choirs, research, and personal stories from choir members.

All proceeds from the sale of this cookbook go directly to the Voices in Motion Choral Society—for the development of future choirs and for ongoing research about the impact of choral music on the lives of people with dementia and their family members.

We invite you to join the movement!

I REMEMBER

I REMEMBER

PRISCILA KUMAR

f you want to start a movement, you begin with children and teenagers. They are our future.

One of the most exciting aspects of Voices in Motion is the inclusion of the younger generation.

They can change and impact our world for the better.

We are on a mission to create a dementia-friendly world and we are pleased that we are having an impact.

Our young people are making a big difference in sharing the message about dementia and talking about it with their peers and family members.

One of our choristers, Priscila Kumar, wrote and illustrated a book entitled *I Remember*. This story is about her experience in the choir, and the narration helps children, as well as adults, understand dementia. In addition, it provides an educational component: a list of questions and answers that facilitate further conversation about dementia.

You can purchase *I Remember* on our website at www.voicesinmotionchoirs.org.

CPSIA information can be obtained
at www.ICGtesting.com
Printed in the USA
JSHW040545251120
9811JS00001B/3